MW00441369

NEVER LOSE
HOPE

Biblical Promises for Times of Trouble, Chaos, and Calamity

CHARLES R.
SWINDOLL

TYNDALE
MOMENTUM®

A Tyndale nonfiction imprint

Visit Tyndale online at tyndale.com.

Visit Tyndale Momentum online at tyndalemomentum.com.

Tyndale, Tyndale's quill logo, *Tyndale Momentum*, and the Tyndale Momentum logo are registered trademarks of Tyndale House Ministries. Tyndale Momentum is a nonfiction imprint of Tyndale House Publishers, Carol Stream, Illinois.

Never Lose Hope: Biblical Promises for Times of Trouble, Chaos, and Calamity

Published in association with Yates & Yates (www.yates2.com).

Unless otherwise indicated, all Scripture quotations are taken from the *Holy Bible*, New Living Translation, copyright © 1996, 2004, 2015 by Tyndale House Foundation. Used by permission of Tyndale House Publishers, Carol Stream, Illinois 60188. All rights reserved.

Scripture quotations marked ESV are from The ESV® Bible (The Holy Bible, English Standard Version®), copyright © 2001 by Crossway, a publishing ministry of Good News Publishers. Used by permission. All rights reserved.

For information about special discounts for bulk purchases, please contact Tyndale House Publishers at csresponse@tyndale.com, or call 1-855-277-9400.

ISBN 978-1-4964-7660-9

Printed in the United States of America

29	28	27	26	25	24	23
7	6	5	4	3	2	1

*May the God of hope fill you with all joy
and peace in believing, so that by the power of
the Holy Spirit you may abound in hope.*

ROMANS 15:13, ESV

Contents

Introduction

WE'RE LIVING IN SOME TOUGH DAYS, FRIENDS. Life is difficult and demanding. It's often filled with pain, heartache, setbacks, and detours. More and more, we seem to be living on the ragged edge of chaos . . .

- one financial crisis away from bankruptcy
- one blowup away from relational collapse

- one temptation away from moral failure
- one calamity away from emotional meltdown
- one illness away from physical breakdown
- one doubt away from apostasy

When such troubles strike, they can be downright devastating. But they don't have to be!

We can endure unexpected calamities. How? By taking our stand on the strong foundation of God's Word. When trials and tribulations rumble in like a fleet of bulldozers to demolish our lives, we can emerge from the rubble with a strong resolve to recover and rebuild. We don't have to settle for merely surviving; we can set our sights on thriving.

Our good, powerful, awesome God is inviting us to run to Him as our only strong tower, which can never teeter or topple.

In Him alone, we can find the strength and hope to endure.

So, fix your eyes on the one who orders chaos, fills emptiness, and lights up the darkness.

When you do, you'll see clearly that there's a purpose at the end of life's journey of adversity.

In fact, more than a purpose—there's a Person.

Trust Him and He will see you through.

Charles R. Swindoll

PROMISES FOR
WHEN TROUBLE
COMES YOUR WAY

◆

Dear brothers and sisters,
when troubles of any kind
come your way, consider it an
opportunity for great joy.

JAMES 1:2

Troubles are inescapable. They come in all shapes and sizes. Some are irksome and irritating, others deep and dangerous. When the inevitable troubles of various kinds come, remember this vital truth about them—*they have a purpose*. They are all part of His plan. When we accept this, we can view them as opportunities for growth. Don't look for an escape hatch. Instead, lean into God's plan and learn from the trials. Let them water your roots so you can grow deeper in your relationship with Him.

◆

We know that God causes everything
to work together for the good of
those who love God and are called
according to his purpose for them.

ROMANS 8:28

Recognizing that troubles have a purpose is
much better than always asking, "Why did
this happen? Why me? Why now?" Instead,
we can ask much more fruitful questions:
"What can I learn from this about God's
grace? About the love of His Son? About the
comfort of the Holy Spirit? What important
truth is God teaching me at this point in
my journey?" When we shift our focus from
"why" to "what," we can begin to face the
inevitable troubles of life as opportunities for
growth and great joy.

◆

"I know the plans I have for you,"
says the LORD. "They are plans for
good and not for disaster,
to give you a future and a hope."

JEREMIAH 29:11

Don't just acknowledge the truth about
God's purpose in our trials; ponder it. Don't
just nod your head in agreement; lean into
it with your whole heart. Remind yourself,
"There's a reason for this difficulty. Through
this, I'll get to know God better. I'll get to
know myself better. Maybe I won't know
exactly how God is working things out for
my good and His glory, but I'm going to
regard it as true." Then remind yourself
again.

◆

The LORD will work out
his plans for my life—
for your faithful love,
O LORD, endures forever.
Don't abandon me,
for you made me.

PSALM 138:8

Let's be honest. We always want the fruits, but we seldom want the fertilizer. We want to reap the wares, but we don't want to pluck the weeds. We want a bountiful harvest of spiritual growth, but we don't love the toil of tilling the rock-hard soil. This is why we need to keep at the forefront of our minds the outcome of this trouble. It's a testing ground for our faith. Through our trials, we reap the greatest spiritual harvest. Knowing this truth will help us endure the challenges we face.

◆

If you need wisdom, ask our
generous God, and he will
give it to you. He will not
rebuke you for asking.

JAMES 1:5

When troubles come and stay, we need to drop to our knees and ask God for the wisdom to handle them. We can pray something like this: "Lord, I'm in a mess, part of which I caused and part of which I didn't. It has brought loss, heartache, feelings of failure, and disappointment to me and to others. I need You to help me see through Your eyes what I can't see through my own. Help me, Lord, to grow through this experience, to look at these troubles from Your perspective. By Your grace, let me ponder it rightly and gain a proper understanding of it. I desperately need Your wisdom because I don't have it in myself." When you ask for wisdom with an honest and sincere heart, you can trust God to answer.

◆

God blesses those who patiently endure testing and temptation. Afterward they will receive the crown of life that God has promised to those who love him.

JAMES 1:12

Not only does God grant us the strength to endure, He also rewards us for that endurance. What grace! When hardships multiply, grace abounds. When our attempts to fix our problems fail, grace keeps us standing. When we handle trials God's way rather than through our own efforts, we receive a sense of contentment, satisfaction, patience, and even deep joy. If we learn to handle life's trials correctly, we'll experience God's blessings.

◆

We can rejoice, too, when we run
into problems and trials, for we know
that they help us develop endurance.
And endurance develops strength of
character, and character strengthens
our confident hope of salvation.
And this hope will not lead to
disappointment. For we know how
dearly God loves us, because he has

given us the Holy Spirit to fill our
hearts with his love.

ROMANS 5:3-5

If we ask God for wisdom to think about
our troubles properly, and if we rely on
His power to endure them, we can go from
wretched souls bruised *by* adversity to wise
souls matured *through* adversity. Trust that
He is working through your troubles for your
good. Let the lingering trial run its course.
Seek His mind as you ask for the wisdom
only He can give. Know that He is at work
to bring you a depth of character you would
otherwise miss.

PROMISES FOR WHEN YOU'RE SICK

◆

I tell you, you can pray for anything,
and if you believe that you've
received it, it will be yours.

MARK 11:24

When suffering makes its mark, one question becomes paramount in people's lives—especially if that suffering comes from ongoing, anguishing pain, debilitating injuries, or a terminal disease. *Does God heal people today?* I believe the Lord our God is a miracle-working God. Nothing is impossible for Him. But before we even ask whether, when, and how God heals, we first need to decide to trust Him when we face sickness or disability . . . regardless of His timing. Trust His goodness. Trust His sovereignty. Let God be God.

◆

He comforts us in all our
troubles so that we can
comfort others.

2 CORINTHIANS 1:4

Maybe you have faced cancer, a stroke, mul-
tiple sclerosis, Parkinson's, or migraines.
Maybe it's a lost job, a bankruptcy, or a mar-
ital betrayal. God comforts us through all
these troubles so our hearts will know how
to reach out to others with comfort. Think
about it. Who better to console the one who
loses a child than someone who's lost a child?
Who better to understand a debilitating sickness than one who has gone through the
same? My son used to have a little sign on
the wall of his office that said, "I've learned
never to trust the words of anyone who has

not gone through serious pain in his or her life." Wise words.

◆

In fact, we expected to die. But
as a result, we stopped relying on
ourselves and learned to rely
only on God, who raises the dead.

2 CORINTHIANS 1:9

When circumstances bring us to the end of ourselves, we're forced to turn to God— whom we should have been depending upon from the start. We learn how much we need Him when we get desperately sick. Sickness develops a full dependence on Him when our hearts are ready to receive it. If God can raise the dead, He can get you through your suffering and sickness, trials and tragedies.

◆

We know that when this earthly
tent we live in is taken down (that
is, when we die and leave this
earthly body), we will have a house
in heaven, an eternal body made
for us by God himself and not by
human hands. . . . So we are always
confident, even though we know that
as long as we live in these bodies we
are not at home with the Lord.

2 CORINTHIANS 5:1, 6

It isn't God's will for everyone to be healed
in this life. I know that's a hard truth. You'll
rarely hear it in contemporary churches.
You'll never hear it from health-and-wealth,
prosperity-gospel preachers. But the fact is,
God never promises that everyone can be

healed physically on this side of eternity. Yet even when we succumb to death, we know that He has sealed us with a promise not only of heaven after death but of a glorious bodily resurrection at the return of Christ.

◆

Be thankful in all circumstances,
for this is God's will for you
who belong to Christ Jesus.

I THESSALONIANS 5:18

As God sees us through suffering, we learn that bitterness isn't the answer. We learn, instead, to give thanks to God for the good days. We thank Him for the little blessings, the promises, the hope of the world to come. When God is working in us, we can pray,

"Thank You, Lord, that even through this suffering You have some purpose beyond my comprehension. You care for me like I never realized before. Thank You for being to me what no one else can ever be. Thank You that sadness may come through the night, but joy comes in the morning. Thank You for Your relief. Thank You for sustaining me. Thank you that I can be a testimony of Your pre-serving grace."

◆

The faithful love of the LORD
never ends! His mercies never cease.
Great is his faithfulness; his mercies
begin afresh each morning.

LAMENTATIONS 3:22-23

God has His reasons for healing some but not healing others—or for healing us at some times but not other times. Regardless of how God chooses to work in our lives, we can trust His goodness and wisdom . . . even in the midst of suffering. When the questions come and the suffering seems too much to bear, cling to the truth that God has a loving purpose in it. He understands your struggles, and He is there with you in the midst of them, providing strength to endure. Look to Him with a thankful heart, and He will see you through!

◆

Whatever is good and perfect is a
gift coming down to us from God
our Father, who created all the lights
in the heavens. He never changes or
casts a shifting shadow.

JAMES 1:17

When healing comes from God, thank Him for it. Receive God's blessing with thankfulness and praise. God can heal us of anything, anytime, anywhere—by any method He chooses. It's all in His sovereign hands. When He chooses *not* to heal—or at least not to heal *immediately*—He doesn't owe us an explanation. He's the Potter; we're the clay. He's the Master; we're the servants. He's God; we're not. Continue to seek Him, to serve Him, and to trust Him.

PROMISES FOR WHEN YOU'RE BURDENED

◆

Don't worry about anything;
instead, pray about everything.
Tell God what you need, and
thank him for all he has done.

PHILIPPIANS 4:6

When we suffer such hardships, what do we do? Pray. Period. Pray for endurance. Pray for insight. Pray for encouragement. Pray for God to intercede. Pray that He'll build bridges to reconciliation, or that He'll provide for your needs. Pray that He'll replace doubt and anxiety with confidence and peace. *Pray!* In the depths of your own crisis, don't hold back. Bombard God's throne with your pleading. The release of anxiety through prayer helps to heal the soul. I can't explain how that works. I just know it does.

◆

Are any of you suffering hardships?
You should pray. Are any of you
happy? You should sing praises.

JAMES 5:13

Life is a mixed bag. We sometimes endure
long autumns of loss or prolonged winters
of suffering. But other times God brings us
through seasons of springtime, when everything comes to life again, or fruitful summers
of bountiful blessing. Some people forget
about God in the good times. They are quick
to blame Him when things go wrong, but
they ignore Him when things go well. Or
they treat Him like a 911 operator, crying out
to Him only in emergencies. As much as you
would bombard heaven with your prayers for
help when suffering, belt out praises toward

heaven with songs of celebration when you are feeling happy.

◆

> Praise the LORD! Praise God in
> his sanctuary; praise him in his
> mighty heaven! Praise him for
> his mighty works; praise his
> unequaled greatness! . . .
> Let everything that breathes
> sing praises to the LORD!

PSALM 150:1-2, 6

Let's be real. Sometimes our days are bright and sunny, sometimes dark and stormy. But most of the time each day has some of each— it's partly cloudy. It starts out cheerful and ends with a crisis. Our days don't roll out in black or white. Most often they linger in the gray. That's all the more reason to sing His praises for those beams of light that pierce the clouds. Joyous praise and thanksgiving are like a balm for the soul. So, let there be praise!

◆

The earnest prayer of a righteous person has great power and produces wonderful results.

JAMES 5:16

Like confession, prayer also provides healing to the soul. Pray when you wake up in the morning, pray when your head hits the pillow at night, and pray throughout the day. Bring everything to the Lord. Pray for others. Ask how you can pray for them. Follow up later to see how God has responded to those prayers. Yes, pray for those who are sick.

Bring your physical concerns to God. He invites that. He wants to hear from you.

◆

We also pray that you will be strengthened with all his glorious power so you will have all the endurance and patience you need.

COLOSSIANS 1:11

When trials roll in, don't fret! We're not on our own. We endure trials because He gives us grace to persevere. He gives endurance. He gives patience. He gives strength. He gives "glorious power." God doesn't toss a ton of trouble on us, coax us with a prod, and shove us on our way through life. He provides everything we need for the trek. Just as God is the source of wisdom for understanding hardships, He's also the source of our strength to endure them.

PROMISES FOR WHEN YOU'RE FACING UNEXPECTED TRIALS

◆

How do you know what your life will
be like tomorrow? Your life is like the
morning fog—it's here a little while,
then it's gone. What you ought
to say is, "If the Lord wants us to,
we will live and do this or that."

JAMES 4:14-15

More often than not, wise living means learn-
ing to roll with the punches. The Bible is clear:
we should neither boast nor fret over tomorrow, because we can never know what's lurking
just around the corner. No wonder James warns
pretentious planners to temper their overcon-
fident business ventures with healthy humility.
If we are to entrust these everyday matters to
God, how much more should we be eager to
entrust our very lives to Him, come what may.

◆

Understand, therefore, that the LORD
your God is indeed God. He is the
faithful God who keeps his covenant
for a thousand generations and lavishes
his unfailing love on those who love
him and obey his commands.

DEUTERONOMY 7:9

There's nothing funny or frivolous about
God's testing. It sometimes feels like He's
pushing us not just to the edge of the cliff but
over the edge—and delighting in it! Yet just
when we think it's "lights out" for us, God
breaks through the silence and says, "I'm right
here with you. I've never left you. I know you
trust Me. You've passed the test!" In those
moments we learn without a doubt that the
Sunday-school God of goodness, sovereignty,

and wisdom is the same God who shows up on those long, dark Mondays that assault our peace of mind and put our theology to the test.

◆

Let us hold tightly without wavering to the hope we affirm, for God can be trusted to keep his promise.

HEBREWS 10:23

In the pages of His Word, we see God at work in the unexpected tests that rattle our world. These trials may feel like pointless detours from God's perfect plan, but God is always working out His perfect will behind the scenes. Pain and heartache often accompany those tests and trials, but in the end, something good invariably comes about for those who endure by God's life-giving grace. We can be confident that He will provide what we need in the midst of it. And He will accomplish His purposes through it.

◆

The temptations in your life are
no different from what others
experience. And God is faithful. He
will not allow the temptation to be
more than you can stand. When
you are tempted, he will show you a
way out so that you can endure.

1 CORINTHIANS 10:13

If you're going through a trial, God has a purpose for it. If you're facing an unexpected test, you can rest on the fact that it's part of God's plan. I've said this several times and I'll say it again, because it's a vital truth of the Christian life that is too easily forgotten. God is completely good, wise, just, and powerful, and He can be trusted to do what's right even when something unexpected rattles your world.

◆

Create in me a clean heart,
O God. Renew a loyal spirit within me.

PSALM 51:10

I've learned over the years that tests and trials are often designed to have us release something we're clutching—a dream, a person, your possessions, a title, or a position. Whatever it is you've been gripping, clinging to, trying in every way to hold onto, let it go. When the unexpected test rattles your world, meet it with faith and obedience. You'll be amazed at the surprising ways God steps in. The path and provision He has for you are so much greater than the ones you're grasping.

PROMISES FOR WHEN YOU'RE FEELING HURT OR BETRAYED

◆

Don't be afraid, for I am with you.
Don't be discouraged, for I am your
God. I will strengthen you and help
you. I will hold you up with my
victorious right hand.

ISAIAH 41:10

Trials are inevitable. So, *don't be surprised*
when they come. Our friends are fallible.
So, *don't be fooled* when well-meaning loved
ones give you bad advice. But our God is
sovereign. So, *don't be disillusioned* when
life hits hard. During the seasons of peace
and blessing, prepare yourself spiritually for
whatever may come. When your life is free
of trouble, don't become complacent. When
calamity crashes in, don't be disillusioned.
He's preparing you to stand before Him,

looking more like His Son than you did at the start.

◆

Be strong and courageous!
Do not be afraid and
do not panic before them.
For the LORD your God will
personally go ahead of you.
He will neither fail you
nor abandon you.

DEUTERONOMY 31:6

Most people have experienced some kind of trauma in their lives. Perhaps you have suffered abuse at the hands of bullies, strangers, or those who were supposed to love and protect you. In the midst of those cruel seasons of suffering and their aftermath, it's certainly easy to wonder, *Where was God?* Yet even in the darkest places, the light of God's grace blazes like a pillar of fire in the night. He intervenes and brings beauty from ugliness, purpose from pain, and comfort from sorrow.

◆

I can never escape from your Spirit!
I can never get away from your
presence! If I go up to heaven, you
are there; if I go down to the grave,
you are there. If I ride the wings
of the morning, if I dwell by the
farthest oceans, even there your
hand will guide me, and your
strength will support me."

PSALM 139:7-10

The promise of God's presence brings needed comfort and encouragement to endure. The first time I grasped the magnitude of this promise was in the Marine Corps. I was on a ship crossing the Pacific Ocean, bound for southeast Asia, and the ocean swells on stormy days were sometimes fifty feet high. It left me feeling alone and uneasy. I remember opening my Bible early one morning to the Psalms, and all thoughts of loneliness and fear fled away. Even though the surrounding swells could have swallowed me up in a moment, that five-word promise—"the Lord is with me"—swept over me with a calming assurance.

◆

If we confess our sins to him,
he is faithful and just to
forgive us our sins and to
cleanse us from all wickedness.

I JOHN 1:9

We're great at reminding ourselves of the wrongs we've done in our own lives. Maybe you can't let yourself forget your failures. Or maybe there's someone you've mistreated or assailed with ugly words. Or maybe you've treated someone unjustly. If you're feeling buried under your own sin, there's no way you can dig yourself out of the hole. Don't even try. Grace can't be earned. God doesn't owe us His blessings, and we couldn't pay Him back for them even if He expected us to. The proper response to God's grace is gratitude.

PROMISES FOR WHEN YOU'RE FACING INSURMOUNTABLE ODDS

◆

You belong to God, my dear
children. You have already won a
victory over those people, because the
Spirit who lives in you is greater than
the spirit who lives in the world.

1 JOHN 4:4

We all deal with "giants" from time to time.
They may not be people; they may be terri-
fying situations, exasperating circumstances,
frightening challenges, or threatening experi-
ences. When we're going through them, they
seem insurmountable. We hear frightening
news or face an overwhelming obstacle, and
our initial response is to size up the situation,
turn heel, and flee in fear. Don't do it! Stand
your ground, knowing that the Spirit of the
living God is with you. The Spirit of life

conquers death itself. Surely, He can deliver you from your "giant."

◆

By his divine power, God has given us everything we need for living a godly life. We have received all of this by coming to know him, the one who called us to himself by means of his marvelous glory and excellence.

2 PETER 1:3

God has outfitted you with everything necessary for victory against the giants you're facing today. He has equipped you with the ever-powerful Spirit of God and all the necessary wisdom, character, virtue, and perseverance only He can give. You're equipped with the One who has never known intimidation or defeat. In fact, He lives within you. And because He's not a Spirit of fear but of power, He can motivate you to get out of your tent of fear and confront whatever oversize obstacles are in your path.

◆

Trust in the LORD with all your
heart; do not depend on your
own understanding. Seek his
will in all you do, and he will
show you which path to take.

PROVERBS 3:5-6

Whenever we're facing a giant, we have to cut through a crowd of voices telling us all the reasons the obstacle is unpassable, the challenge unbeatable, or the bond unbreakable. Often, the voice is in our own heads. Sometimes it comes from people we love and respect. Other times it comes from opponents who want to see us living in defeat (like *they* are). If we listen to those voices telling us what *can't* be done, we've lost the battle even before it's begun. Instead, listen to God's voice in His Word.

◆

I can do everything through Christ,
who gives me strength.

PHILIPPIANS 4:13

What are you going to do when the giants of life attack? Let me speak from my lifetime of experience. You can't beat walking by faith. You can't beat stepping into the battle in the strength of the Lord. You can't beat ignoring the vocal majority who give you bad advice. Don't get swept up by the voices of the crowd.

Don't hide out in a tent of fear and excuses like King Saul did when he cowered from Goliath. Instead, gather stones of faith like David, then watch God work to slay your giant and lead you to victory.

PROMISES FOR WHEN YOU'RE FEELING IMPATIENT

◆

God is pleased when, conscious of his will,
you patiently endure unjust treatment. . . .
For God called you to do good, even if it
means suffering, just as Christ suffered for you.

1 PETER 2:19, 21

We often call God the Great Physician—and
He certainly is. God never runs out of treat-
ments for our sin-sickness, regardless of its specific symptoms. He often uses unpleasant and
painful circumstances on our road to spiritual
fitness. He teaches us trust by reminding us
how helpless we are. He teaches us patience by
making us wait for what we want. He teaches
us obedience by allowing us to experience the
consequences of sin. He teaches us wisdom by
allowing us to fail and make mistakes.

◆

Don't copy the behavior and customs
of this world, but let God transform
you into a new person by changing
the way you think. Then you will
learn to know God's will for you,
which is good and pleasing and
perfect.

ROMANS 12:2

Let's be honest. When it becomes clear God
is not going to take our suffering away, we
often lower our gaze from Him and instead
spill our guts to people around us. *We need to
quit complaining about our pain.* We need to
stop begging over and over for relief. God has
heard your prayers. He knows your desires.
Our incessant obsessing over our pain may

be short-circuiting what God is trying to teach us. Instead of complaining endlessly, we need to lift our eyes to Him. To find His strength in our weakness. To lean into His sustaining grace.

◆

Have you forgotten the encouraging
words God spoke to you as his
children? He said, "My child, don't
make light of the LORD's discipline,
and don't give up when he corrects
you. For the LORD disciplines those
he loves, and he punishes each one
he accepts as his child."

HEBREWS 12:5-6

As God's children, we can rest all our confi-dence in the fact that God the Father knows best. He knows what to give us, what to keep from us, and how much we can handle as He seeks to accomplish His purpose of keeping us humbly dependent on Him. The Lord has specific trials with our names on them. They're designed for us, arranged with our weaknesses and maturity levels in mind. He bears down and doesn't let up. Yet He's always in control, making sure the trials are no more and no less than we need. Yes, we groan and weep. But we also learn and grow.

◆

That is why we never give up.
Though our bodies are dying, our
spirits are being renewed every day.
For our present troubles are small
and won't last very long. Yet they
produce for us a glory that vastly
outweighs them and will last forever!

So we don't look at the troubles we
can see now; rather, we fix our gaze
on things that cannot be seen. For
the things we see now will soon
be gone, but the things we cannot
see will last forever."

2 CORINTHIANS 4:16-18

The Lord sometimes uses painful events
and chronic suffering to mold us and fashion us into the image of His Son. He may
use intense troubles to reveal behaviors that
need to change. He may send ongoing trials to make you aware of attitudes that need
adjustment. It may seem like He's crushing
you, but He's curing you. It may feel like He's
harming you, but He's healing you. It may
look like He hates you, but He loves you.
He's calling you to attention and turning you
away from yourself and toward His Son.

◆

We ask God to give you complete
knowledge of his will and to give you
spiritual wisdom and understanding.
Then the way you live will always
honor and please the Lord, and your
lives will produce every kind of good
fruit. All the while, you will grow as
you learn to know God
better and better.

COLOSSIANS 1:9-10

The training ground of life designed for God's
children includes suffering. In this lifelong
training, the great Teacher knows you thor-
oughly and loves you unconditionally. You
can trust Him. You can trust His process. If
you stick with it, you'll eventually see signs
that you're growing. You'll grasp principles

you never understood before. You'll gain insight into yourself and others. You'll go deeper into the truths of God. But only if you keep walking the path He has for you.

PROMISES FOR WHEN YOU'RE FEELING DISAPPOINTED

◆

You can make many plans, but the
Lord's purpose will prevail.

PROVERBS 19:21

A lot of life's letdowns have a greater purpose. That five-minute delay looking for
your misplaced car key? Maybe the Lord
kept you out of a deadly accident on your
commute. That part-time job you didn't get
when you were in college? Maybe the Lord
steered you away from a wrong career path.
That date who stood you up and made you
feel so small all those years ago? Maybe it was
God's way of keeping you available for the
person He had in mind for you to meet and
later marry. Trust in God's wisdom, goodness, and sovereignty.

◆

I am certain that God, who
began the good work within you,
will continue his work until it is
finally finished on the day when
Christ Jesus returns.

PHILIPPIANS 1:6

Maybe you find yourself in circumstances
where your potential is hampered by limi-
tations beyond your control. Look again.
What open doors might you be overlooking
right in front of your nose? God may be
using the closed doors to accomplish certain results in your life—or to equip you
for something much larger. They may be
turning your attention away from yourself
and back to God. Maybe He's teaching you

to trust Him completely, to wait on Him patiently, and to surrender to Him and His timing entirely.

◆

You will show me the way of
life, granting me the joy of your
presence and the pleasures of
living with you forever.

PSALM 16:11

I'm convinced that you and I spend too much of our lives staring at closed doors. We're dejected, disappointed, maybe even offended that God wouldn't let us through. We make our plans, plot our courses, and push off with enthusiasm—only to be way-laid by some insurmountable obstacle that sends us back to square one. The truth is, sometimes God closes doors to the logical, easy path to open us up to opportunities we've viewed as insurmountable.

◆

The LORD is my strength and
shield. I trust him with all my
heart. He helps me, and my heart
is filled with joy. I burst out in
songs of thanksgiving.

PSALM 28:7

I find great comfort in knowing God is God and I am not. The longer I've lived, the less put off I am when God slams doors shut and moves me in another direction. Yes, early on in life and ministry it irritated me. I'd sometimes pout, maybe even grumble. But I finally discovered He always opens new doors of opportunity I could never have imagined. I'm not at all offended when a good, all-wise, sovereign God steers me in a better direction. In fact, I'm grateful. And you should be too.

◆

Seek the Kingdom of God above all else, and live righteously, and he will give you everything you need.

MATTHEW 6:33

Stop pounding on closed doors. Stop trying to pry them open. Leave them with God. Know that God takes full responsibility for the doors He closes to you and those He opens. He can—and will—deal with what's behind them in His own way. You don't need to worry about them. The door

God closes to you may be opened for some-
body else. That's His business. Move along,
knowing that the Lord will guide you where
He needs you.

◆

Blessed are those who trust in the
LORD and have made the LORD their
hope and confidence. They are like
trees planted along a riverbank, with
roots that reach deep into the water.
Such trees are not bothered by the
heat or worried by long months of
drought. Their leaves stay green, and
they never stop producing fruit.

JEREMIAH 17:7-8

When God closes a door, it doesn't neces-
sarily mean your plan was bad. It doesn't

always mean He's keeping you from evil or from danger. It may very well be that He's steering you away from something that would have been good . . . but where He leads you instead is much better. So, when God closes the door on something you know would be good, brace yourself. He may have something even greater in mind. Trust in Him with firm hope and confidence, and in due season His plans for you will bear fruit.

PROMISES FOR WHEN
YOU'RE FEELING ALONE

◆

When you pray, go away by yourself,
shut the door behind you, and pray to
your Father in private. Then your Father,
who sees everything, will reward you.

MATTHEW 6:6

For many of us, being alone feels like a punishment. But maybe we should be looking at times of solitude as opportunities for in-depth self-examination. The change of pace, the silence, the solace—these provide an ideal context for cultivating greater awareness of where we really are spiritually . . . and where God wants us to be. Times of solitude afford an occasion to push pause on our high-speed existence. To look within. To ask, "Lord, is there anything in my life that needs special attention?"

◆

Search me, O God, and know my
heart; test me and know my anxious
thoughts. Point out anything in me
that offends you, and lead me along
the path of everlasting life.

PSALM 139:23-24

David invited the Lord to probe his life—to
shine light on the deepest, darkest crevices
of his heart and mind. In our alone times
with God, we need to make that prayer our
own. When we have a spiritual oasis, God
often opens our eyes to blights on our character that require confession and cleans-
ing. Afterward, when the Spirit of God has
restored our soul, we can experience victory
over our deepest struggles in the journey
toward Christlikeness.

◆

Let the Spirit renew your thoughts
and attitudes. Put on your new
nature, created to be like God—
truly righteous and holy.

EPHESIANS 4:23-24

As uncomfortable as it may be to hear, God will sometimes orchestrate your circumstances for the sole purpose of stopping you in your tracks. What does God want from you during those periods when your life has slowed down or come to a sudden halt? He wants you to do what you're always supposed to do: He wants you to make the most of the time you have. He wants you to grow deeper in every way as He shapes you to become more and more like Christ. He wants you to allow the Spirit to fashion in you godly traits of Christlike character.

◆

Before daybreak the next morning,
Jesus got up and went out to an
isolated place to pray.

MARK 1:35

Just as solitude was necessary for Jesus, it's equally necessary for us. We owe it to ourselves, to God, and to those around us to withdraw, as Jesus did, and find solace in silence. Perhaps you shake your head and wonder, "What in the world would I do in all that silence and solitude?" To begin with, you pray. You sit and think in silence. You meditate on selected Scriptures. You consider the thoughts and struggles of your heart. You reflect on your responses and attitudes. And you let the Lord probe your soul.

◆

Your word is a lamp to guide my feet
and a light for my path.

PSALM 119:105

Make the most of your times of solitude. Spill out your heart to Him in prayer, yes, but also listen to His illuminating voice through His Word. Rather than grinding your teeth in irritation during times of solitude, treasure these moments as a gift. Only God knows the plans He has for *you*. Set aside those times to be alone with Him. Listen to His voice. You'll delve into deep truths and explore new heights of unimaginable glory. All you need to do is embrace the solitude, take His hand, and let Him lead you.

PROMISES FOR WHEN YOU'RE WONDERING IF GOD IS THERE

◆

Job stood up and tore his robe in grief.
Then he shaved his head and fell to the
ground to worship. He said, "I came naked
from my mother's womb, and I will be
naked when I leave. The LORD gave me
what I had, and the LORD has taken it away.
Praise the name of the LORD!"

JOB 1:20-21

In a moment, Job lost everything that
mattered—his livelihood, his heirs, his
social standing, and finally his health. The
God whom he had loved and worshiped all
his life seemed not just silent but absent. Job
could easily have slipped into thoughts he
had never entertained before: *Where is God?
Why does He seem so distant? Does He even
care? Does He even exist?* How easy for us to

slip into a similar pattern of thinking, wondering if God is really there. In times like that, we must rest on the foundational truth that the Lord gives and takes away—for our good and His glory. He never leaves you—especially in the darkest days.

◆

Be still, and know that I am God!

PSALM 46:10

God doesn't always show a clear path forward. Often, He keeps us in a holding pattern for weeks, months—even years. We may never get a clear explanation for why God wanted us to move in direction B instead of direction A. So it is in the life of faith. God works in strange, unexpected, and mysterious ways. And He may use surprising methods to steer our course. But we need to keep moving. God will open and close doors by His sovereign hand. In those seasons, it may seem as if God isn't really there. But take comfort in knowing He is always working in His own ways and according to His own timing.

◆

The wisdom from above is first of all pure. It is also peace loving, gentle at all times, and willing to yield to others. It is full of mercy and the fruit of good deeds. It shows no favoritism and is always sincere.

JAMES 3:17

How we need wisdom from above! Sometimes we get so caught up in our misery that we forget to stop, step back, and ask, "What does

God want to teach me through this?" How easy it is to lose sight of the lessons God has for us in every situation. I can't help but wonder if most of us completely miss the message God has for us in our circumstances. It's easy to overlook in the seemingly disjointed, random, unexpected happenings in our lives—forgetting that God does, indeed, work all these things together for our good. We need wisdom from on high to recognize that God is ever-present in the seemingly disjointed events of life.

◆

I am the vine; you are the branches. Those who remain in me, and I in them, will produce much fruit. For apart from me you can do nothing.

JOHN 15:5

Each person has a unique combination of talents, personality, abilities, strengths, resources, and opportunities. Without being plugged into Him as the source of our spiritual power, we'll produce nothing worthwhile, nothing worthy of eternal reward, nothing that will have true, lasting impact. Only the fruit borne by the power of the Spirit in the name of Christ will be deemed authentic.

About the Author

CHARLES R. SWINDOLL is the founder and senior pastor–teacher of Stonebriar Community Church in Frisco, Texas. But Chuck's listening audience extends far beyond a local church body, as Insight for Living airs on major Christian radio markets around the world. Chuck's extensive writing ministry has also served the body of Christ worldwide, and his leadership as president and now chancellor of Dallas Theological Seminary has helped prepare and equip a new generation of men and women for ministry. Chuck and his wife, Cynthia, his partner in life and ministry, have four grown children and seven great grandchildren.